TATER
Folks

MARGARET R. EDINBURGH

AuthorHouse™
1663 Liberty Drive
Bloomington, IN 47403
www.authorhouse.com
Phone: 833-262-8899

Because of the dynamic nature of the Internet, any web addresses or links contained in this book may have changed since publication and may no longer be valid. The views expressed in this work are solely those of the author and do not necessarily reflect the views of the publisher, and the publisher hereby disclaims any responsibility for them.

Illustrations by: Aquina Parker

This book is printed on acid-free paper.

ISBN: 978-1-6655-3859-6 (sc)
ISBN: 978-1-6655-3861-9 (hc)
ISBN: 978-1-6655-3860-2 (e)

Print information available on the last page.

Published by AuthorHouse 12/06/2021

authorHOUSE®

DEDICATION

This book is dedicated to my daughter, Tomiyko. She is my constant companion, always there to support me. It is also a tribute to my late mother and sister, Charlieveen and Ella Edinburgh. The two of them were my biggest fans. It is dedicated to those friends and family members who have supported me along this journey. Finally, it is dedicated to my generations of nieces and nephews, those I know, those I don't know and those who are yet to come.

PREFACE

This is Margaret Rose Edinburgh's note to parents, guardians, teachers, and anyone who cares for children. This story has been told over and over again by numerous different folks. It was originally a children's sermon. At this point in time, the original author is unknown. Many who tell the story call it, "Tator People." I have chosen to retell the story, making it an adaptive work. I have chosen to title it, "Tater Folk." One may use the names given to the characters in this book are all nouns. A noun is the name given to a person, place, or thing. It is the subject of a verb.

After working as an administrator for all of my adult life, my purpose for sharing this adaptive work is teaching about the different types of folks one may find in any work environment, social club, or place where folks come together to complete a project.

TATER FOLKS

Some folks...

Some folks never seem motivated to participate but are just content to watch while others do the work.

They are called "Spec Tators."

SPECTATOR

(spec-ta-ter) Noun

An observer of an event.

SOME FOLKS...

Some folks never do anything to help, but they are gifted at finding fault with the way others do the work.

They are called "Comment Tators."

COMMENTATOR

(kom-men-ta-ter) Noun

1. A broadcaster or writer who reports and analyzes events in the news.

2. One who writes or delivers a commentary or commentaries.

SOME FOLKS...

Some folks are very bossy and like to tell others what to do, but don't want to soil their own hands.

They are called "Dick Tators."

DICTATOR

(dik-ta-ter) Noun

An absolute ruler.

A tyrant; a despot.

DESPOT

(\ ˈde-spot) Noun

A person who uses power or authority in a cruel, unjust, or harmful way.

SOME FOLKS...

Some folks are always looking to cause problems by asking others to agree with them.

It is too hot or too cold, too sour or too sweet.

They are called "Agie Tators."

AGITATOR

(agi-ta-tor) Noun

Noun: One who agitates, especially one who engages in political agitation.

YOU KNOW SOME FOLKS...

There are those who say they will help, but somehow just never get around to actually delivering the promised help.

They are called "Hezzie Tators."

HESITATOR

(hez-zie-tater) Noun

Noun: to stop because of indecision; pause or delay in acting, choosing, or deciding because of feeling unsure; waiver

SOME FOLKS...

Some folks can put up a front and pretend to be someone they are not.

They are called "Emma Tators."

IMITATORS

(im-i-ta-tor) Noun

To act the same as; impersonate; mimic; copy

YOU KNOW SOME FOLKS...

Then there are those who love others and do what they say they will. They are always prepared to stop whatever they are doing and lend a helping hand. They bring real sunshine into the lives of others.

They are called "Sweet Tators."

SWEET TATOR

(sw-eet ta-ter) Noun

Slang for a person who always does nice things for others